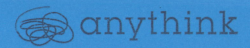

Essential Life Science

ADAPTATION

Melanie Waldron

Heinemann
LIBRARY

Chicago, Illinois

To contact Capstone Global Library, please call 800-747-4992, or visit our web site, www.capstonepub.com

Edited by Nancy Dickmann and Abby Colich
Designed by Rich Parker
Original illustrations © Capstone Global
    Library Ltd 2013
Illustrated by HL Studio
Picture research by Tracy Cummins
Originated by Capstone Global Library Ltd
Printed in China by China Translation and
    Printing Services

17 16 15 14 13
10 9 8 7 6 5 4 3 2 1

Library of Congress Cataloging-in-Publication Data
Waldron, Melanie.
  Adaptation / Melanie Waldron.
    pages cm—(Essential life science)
  Includes bibliographical references and index.
  ISBN 978-1-4329-7805-1 (hb)—ISBN 978-1-4329-7837-2 (pb) 1. Adaptation (Biology)—Juvenile literature. I. Title.

  QH546.W26 2014
  578.4—dc23   2012046445

Acknowledgments
We would like to thank the following for permission to reproduce photographs: Capstone Library: pp. 10 (Karon Dubke), 11 (Karon Dubke), 16 (Karon Dubke), 17 (Karon Dubke), 36 (Karon Dubke), 37 (Karon Dubke); Getty Images: pp. 4 (© 2012 The Photography Factory), 8 (Nigel Pavitt), 13 (altrendo travel), 14 (Oliver Gerhard), 19 (Daniel Cox), 31 (Joe Cornish), 42 (Joel Sartore); Istockphoto: p. 21 (© technotr); Photo Researchers, Inc.: pp. 5 (Philippe Psaila), 9 (Thomas & Pat Leeson), 22 (Nature's Images), 23 (Carlyn Iverson), 26 (F. Stuart Westmorland), 27 (Christopher Swann), 28 (Gregory G. Dimijian), 38 (Eye of Science), 40 (Rafael Macia), 41 (Steve Maslowski), 43 (Francois Gohier); Shutterstock: pp. 7 (© Tischenko Irina), 15 (© Kjersti Joergensen), 24 (© samarttiw), 33 (© papkin), 35 (© Piotr Wawrzyniuk); Superstock: pp. 18 (© NHPA), 25 (© NHPA), 29 (© Minden Pictures), 32 (© Frank van Egmond / age fotostock), 34 (© NaturePL).

Cover photograph of a brown-throated, three-toed sloth reproduced with permission from Superstock (© Minden Pictures).

Every effort has been made to contact copyright holders of material reproduced in this book. Any omissions will be rectified in subsequent printings if notice is given to the publisher.

Contents

Eureka moment!

Learn about important discoveries that have brought about further knowledge and understanding.

DID YOU KNOW?

Discover fascinating facts about adaptation.

WHAT'S NEXT?

Read about the latest research and advances in essential life science.

Some words are shown in bold, **like this**. You can find out what they mean by looking in the glossary.

What Lives in Our Diverse World?

Think for a minute about your backyard, or a local park or nature area. Think about all the different plants growing there. If you looked closely enough among these plants, you would also find a lot of different animals living there. The more different types of plants and animals in an area, the more **diverse** it is.

All the plants and animals have found a way of living there. They are all perfectly **adapted** to their environment.

A diverse world

Now think about all the different places in the world where plants and animals can live. Even the driest deserts and the deepest oceans have things living there.

There is a huge variety of plants across the world, with different animals living around them.

There are all sorts of strange and wonderful plants and animals living all around the world. Each one has adapted to living in its environment. Some live in places where no humans would survive, and very few other plants and animals would survive. Others live in places where lots of other things live.

The olm is an **amphibian** that has adapted to live deep in caves. It is blind — because there is no light where it lives, it does not need eyes. It can live to be 100 years old!

What Is Adaptation?

Adaptation is how a plant or animal finds a way to survive in its **habitat**—the area where it lives. There are lots of different habitats across the world. Similar ones can be grouped together to form Earth's **biomes**. These are areas with similar **climates** and where similar plants and animals live. In each biome and each habitat, plants and animals find different ways to survive.

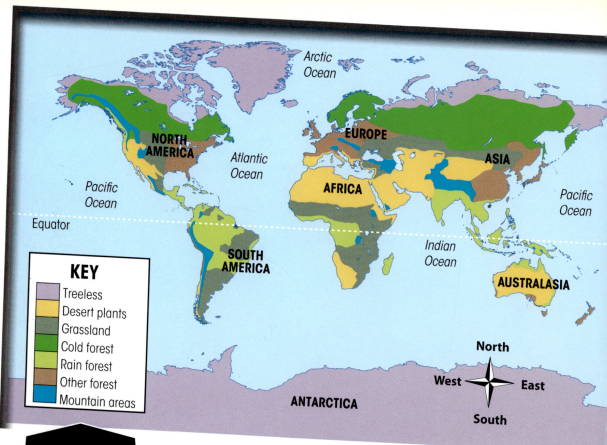

KEY
- Treeless
- Desert plants
- Grassland
- Cold forest
- Rain forest
- Other forest
- Mountain areas

Arctic Ocean

NORTH AMERICA

Atlantic Ocean

Pacific Ocean

Equator

EUROPE

ASIA

AFRICA

Pacific Ocean

SOUTH AMERICA

Indian Ocean

AUSTRALASIA

North
West — East
South

ANTARCTICA

This map shows Earth's biomes.

What do plants and animals need to survive?

Both plants and animals need energy. Plants get their energy from sunlight. They use this to make their own food. Animals need to eat food—either plants or other animals—to get their energy. Plants and animals also need water to survive.

Animals need to breathe **oxygen**, and plants also need oxygen. Most animals need some shelter, to give protection from the weather and to hide from **predators**.

Oxygen is not just in the air! It dissolves in water, so fish can get all the oxygen they need from the sea.

Surviving to breed

Most animals want to make sure that they can breed. This means mating with another animal and having offspring—baby animals that will grow into adults. Plants also have offspring. Most plants do this by making seeds, which can grow into new plants.

Eureka moment!

Charles Darwin was a British scientist in the 1800s. He studied lots of different types of animals and was the first to explain how they became adapted to their environments.

Natural selection

Over time, as environments and habitats have changed, plants and animals have adapted to change with them. Plants and animals that adapt better are able to survive and breed new plants and animals. This is called **natural selection**. It means that only the plants and animals that are best suited to their environment will survive.

Types of adaptation

There are different types of adaptation. The most obvious adaptation is the way a plant or animal looks—the shape, size, and color of it. For example, seals have sleek, long bodies. This shape helps them to swim through water.

The dragon's blood tree grows on hot, dry islands in the Arabian Sea. Its shape helps it to catch and funnel every drop of rain that lands on it. The thick canopy also shades the roots from the sun.

Changing behavior

Some animals have adapted by changing the way they behave. Behavior includes what they do, and how they do it. For example, honeybees can tell other bees where to find nectar by doing "dancing" movements in the hive.

The way an animal's body reacts to something is another type of adaptation. For example, a suntan is how skin reacts to sunlight. The tan is the skin trying to defend itself against harmful rays.

Eureka moment!

In 2009 researchers discovered that some octopuses can use tools! They can gather up coconut shells from the seabed. They carry these around, then hide under them when they feel threatened.

This sea otter has learned to use a rock to help it open a clam shell.

Try This!

Your body can adapt to changing conditions. Try this experiment to see how your body responds.

Prediction

My body will adapt to cope with changing conditions.

What you need

- jump rope
- warm clothing
- paper
- pen

What you do

1. You need to make your body hot. Do this by exercising for about ten minutes. Jogging or skipping are good ways to make you feel hot. Wear warm clothes while you do this.

2. Your body will begin to feel warm as you exercise. What does this make you want to do? Do you want to add more layers of clothes, or take some off? Do you want to have a warm drink or a cold drink? How does your skin feel? Write down how you feel.

3 Now try to get your body to cool down. You could sit very still in front of a fan, for example.

4 As you begin to feel cold, notice what your body does. What do you want to do? Do you want to take your clothes off, or add more layers? Do you want to drink an ice-cold drink or a warm drink? Write down how you feel.

Conclusion

Your body responds to warming up by sweating. This is an adaptation to help your body temperature stay level. You also want to take off some layers and have a cold drink—these are behavioral adaptations.

Your body also responds to cooling down. If you get very cold, you might start to shiver. This is an adaptation to maintain your body temperature. You feel like putting more clothes on and having a warm drink—these are also behavioral adaptations.

How Do Living Things Adapt to Heat?

Some of Earth's habitats are very hot. The rain forests around the world have lots of plants and animals living there. The climate is hot and wet, and this produces lush green forest. Hot, dry deserts sometimes look like nothing can live there, but some plants and animals have adapted to these conditions.

Hot deserts are Earth's hottest, driest areas. Rain forests are also hot, but they get a lot of rainfall.

EUROPE

NORTH AMERICA

ASIA

Pacific Ocean

Tropic of Cancer

Pacific Ocean

Atlantic Ocean

AFRICA

Equator

SOUTH AMERICA

Indian Ocean

AUSTRALASIA

Tropic of Capricorn

☐ Hot Deserts
☐ Rain forests

ANTARCTICA

Water

The main problem in deserts is the lack of water. Plants have developed clever ways to cope with this. Many plants have thick, waxy leaves. This helps to stop them from losing water through the leaves. Some plants, like cactus plants, can store water in their thick **stems**.

Animals must find water to survive too. Some travel huge distances to find water, and remember these places for the future. The fog-basking beetle stands on top of sand dunes. As fog drifts over the dunes, little droplets of water form on its back and run down into its mouth. Desert honey ants have abdomens that can blow up really big. They store food and water in them.

WHAT'S NEXT?

People living in dry areas use different ways to get water. Some use huge nets that capture water droplets from fog, just like fog-basking beetles.

The camel can shut its nostrils, keeping out sand.

The camel's long, thick eyelashes keep out the sand.

The camel stores fat here, which is broken down to make water and energy when the camel needs it.

The camel can drink up to 35 gallons (135 liters) of water in one go! This will last it about a week, and then it must drink again.

The camel's feet spread its weight and stop it from sinking into the sand.

Camels are ideally adapted to living and traveling in deserts.

Rain forest plant adaptations

Plants grow so well in hot, wet rain forests that their main problem is finding the space to grow! They also need to compete with each other to get as much sunlight as possible.

Emergents are trees that grow taller and faster than other trees, and so can stick out above the roof of the forest, catching sunlight. Epiphytes are plants that don't grow out of the ground. They grow high up on the branches of trees, reaching sunlight. Climbers use other plants to grow up and around. Some plants have enormous leaves to catch as much light as possible.

DID YOU KNOW?

The giant taro plant has some of the largest leaves in the world. The leaves try to catch as much light in the rain forest as possible. The plant's stem and roots can be peeled and boiled just like a potato, and over 300 million people around the world eat taro plants!

These epiphytes are growing high on a tree trunk, catching as much light as possible.

Rain forest animal adaptations

Lots of different animals live in rain forests. Some have **camouflage** so they can hide from predators. Others use color in a different way. They are brightly colored, to warn animals that they are poisonous.

Many rain forest animals have strong front arms to help them climb trees. Some have tails that act almost like a third arm or leg—they can twist and hold onto tree branches. Goeldi's monkeys, in the Amazon rain forest, have curved claws to help them cling onto tree trunks.

oths have little grooves in eir fur hairs where algae can ow. This gives the oth camouflage.

Try This!

Plants living in hot, dry areas must hold onto their water! Water can come out of plant leaves and turn into a gas called water vapor, escaping into the air. This is called **evaporating**. Try this experiment to see how some adaptations can reduce evaporation.

Prediction

Water poured into a wide tray will evaporate more quickly than the same amount of water in a cup. Covering the water with a layer of oil will help stop evaporation.

What you need

- water
- shallow tray (about the size of a small book)
- measuring cup
- two cups or mugs
- teaspoon of ordinary cooking oil

What you do:

(1) Pour water into the shallow tray until it is about half an inch (1 cm) deep. Make a note of how much water this is.

(2) Pour the same amount of water into each cup. Carefully pour the oil onto the water in one cup, trying to keep two separate layers.

3 If the weather is warm and dry, place the tray and cups outside. If not, place them in a warm room.

4 Keep checking on the tray and cups over the next few days. Which one dries up first?

Conclusion

The water in the shallow tray dried up more quickly than the water in the cups. This is because more of the water in the tray was exposed to the warm air, so it evaporated more quickly. The water covered by the oil dried up slowest, because the oil prevented some of the water from evaporating.

Some plants in hot, dry areas have very small, fleshy leaves. This means that less leaf area is exposed to the hot air, so the leaves lose less water. Some plants have a waxy coating on their leaves. This acts like the oil to stop evaporation.

How Do Living Things Adapt to Cold?

In the cold areas of the world it is harder for animals to keep warm, find food, and find shelter. Plants have to cope with the cold too.

Staying warm

Penguins and sea **mammals** such as seals live in the Antarctic. They have adapted to the cold by having layers of fat under their skin. In the Arctic, animals such as walruses also have fat layers. Some land animals, such as polar bears, have thick fur.

Emperor penguins must survive freezing temperatures in Antarctica. One behavioral adaptation they have developed is to huddle closely together, sharing each other's body warmth.

Animal adaptations

Animals living in cold areas where there is very little shelter need to hide from predators. Many use camouflage to do this.

Some animals **migrate** in winter. This means that they walk or fly to warmer areas, where there is also more food. Some birds migrate over huge distances. For example, the Arctic tern migrates between the Arctic and the Antarctic! They do this so they can fish all day long, year-round.

One type of fish swimming in cold waters has adapted by having a chemical in its blood that stops it from freezing. The Antarctic toothfish moves very slowly and has a very slow heartbeat, saving energy.

DID YOU KNOW?

The woolly bear caterpillar freezes solid every winter! In spring, it thaws out and becomes active again. It takes 14 years for it to become ready to change into a moth. When this happens, it has only a few days to breed before it dies.

In winter, the Arctic fox grows white fur. This gives it good camouflage against the snow.

Plants in cold areas

Plants in the Arctic have to cope with high winds, so they grow low to the ground. Most plants grow slowly. Some trees can grow around the edges of the Arctic, though the soils here freeze below a certain level. Trees in some areas of the Arctic are **evergreen**, so they can make food in their leaves year-round. Their leaves and sap contain a chemical that stops them from freezing.

Mountain plants

In mountain regions, plants have adapted to the cold weather, strong winds, and steep slopes. Plants combat the cold with chemicals to stop them from freezing. They often have hairy stems to trap warm air, and waxy leaves to stop the wind from drying them out.

Mountain ranges can have several different habitat types, from gentle **foothills** to bare **summits**. Different plants and animals have adapted to live in different zones.

bare rock, ice, and snow: few plants and animals

thin soil, steep, cold climate: moss, lichen, and small plants

less steep, cold climate: meadows and grassland

slightly warmer climate: coniferous trees

thick soil, gentle slopes, warmer climate: deciduous trees

thick soil, hot and wet climate: rain forest (in tropical areas)

Mountain animals

Mountain sheep and goats have small, sharp hooves for walking around on steep rocky areas. Most have thick fur to keep them warm. Mountain insects fly low to the ground, to stop the wind from blowing them away.

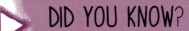

This ibex has small, tough hooves and thick fur.

How Do Plants and Animals Live in Freshwater?

Ponds, lakes, rivers, and streams are all freshwater, not salty like the sea. Different plants and animals have adapted to live in freshwater.

Getting oxygen

Animals living in freshwater need to get oxygen. Some have adapted by having **gills**. These are feathery body parts that can take oxygen from water as it passes over them. Some animals can take oxygen in through the skin on their bodies. Some animals live in water, but come to the surface to breathe air.

These mosquito larvae hang from the surface of the water, breathing air through the tube they hang from.

Going with the flow

In rivers and streams, animals have to cope with the flowing water, otherwise they would be swept along with the water. Different animals have adapted different ways of staying put. Most fish have long, narrow bodies, so the water can easily flow past them. Some fish, such as loaches, have suckers on their front fins. They use these to stick themselves to rocks. Tiny animals can burrow into the mud on the river bottom, and some animals stay close to the bottom of the river, avoiding the faster-flowing water above them.

WHAT'S NEXT?

Scientists have discovered that rivers made by melting glaciers contain lots of tiny animals that are adapted to the cold water. They are worried that **global warming** might mean that some glaciers disappear completely. This would mean that these tiny animals would also disappear.

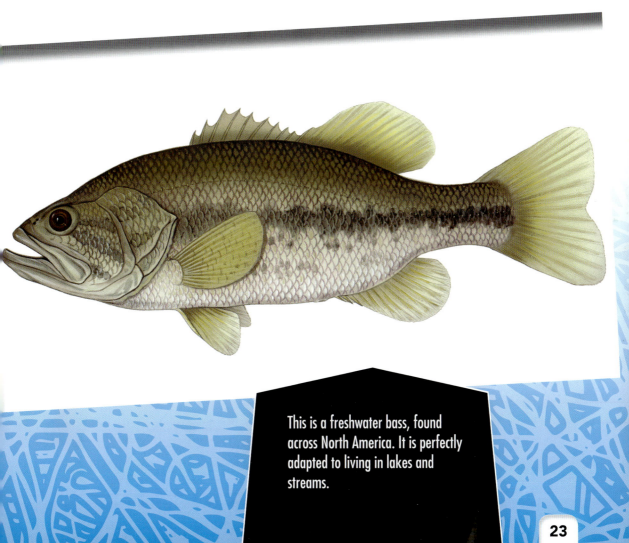

This is a freshwater bass, found across North America. It is perfectly adapted to living in lakes and streams.

How do plants grow in water?

Most plants growing in freshwater have their roots in the mud and gravel at the bottom. This stops them from being swept away by the water. Plants with leaves under the water usually have feathery leaves, to stop the water from dragging on them too much. Some have leaves that float on the surface of the water, or stick up above the surface, to catch as much light as possible. Some plants, such as duckweed, do not have roots in the ground. They float freely on the surface of the water.

Water lily leaves float on the surface of the water, so they can catch lots of sunlight.

Catching food

Some freshwater animals, such as pike, hide among plants. Their bodies are camouflaged to help them hide. They lie in wait to catch their **prey** as it swims by. Caddisfly larvae spin little nets to trap tiny animals. Giant water bugs grab their prey with their strong claws.

Archerfish have a different adaptation to help them catch their food. They spit jets of water at insects flying above the river surface. The insects fall onto the water, and the archerfish eats them up.

WHAT'S NEXT?

Lake Ellsworth is a huge lake lying deep below thick ice in the Antarctic. Scientists are drilling down through the ice to reach the water. They are hoping to discover some living things. They are not sure if anything can survive in this hidden lake.

Duck-billed platypuses hunt for food using their bills. These contain sensors that can detect movement in the water.

How Have Sea Plants and Animals Adapted?

The sea covers around 70 percent of Earth's surface. For seawater plants, the main problem is getting enough light. Light can reach down into the sea's top layers, but below 330 feet (100 meters) there is almost no light at all, so no plants can grow.

Above 330 feet (100 meters), however, plants can grow well. Phytoplankton are tiny, floating, plant-like organisms that are perfectly adapted to growing in the ocean. They keep themselves afloat by having flattened shapes, spines, and hairs that act like parachutes. Lots of sea creatures eat phytoplankton. Large seaweeds, such as kelps and wracks, adapt to the moving tides and currents by having **holdfasts** to grip onto rocks.

Some animals, such as sea anemones, hold onto rocks. They wait for the moving water to bring food to them.

Sea mammals

Mammals living in the sea, such as whales, need to come to the surface to breathe air. Some sea mammals choose to dive deep to find their food. When Weddell seals dive, the high pressure of the seawater makes their lungs collapse. The oxygen gets stored in their muscles.

DID YOU KNOW?

Whales and dolphins have to come to the surface to breathe, so they have to think about when they need to take a breath. This is a problem when it comes to sleeping. Biologists think they get around this by only letting half of their brains sleep at one time, so they are always able to think about taking a breath.

Baleen whales do not have teeth. They have bristles, called baleen. These filter out huge amounts of plankton from seawater, which they scoop into their mouths.

Huge animals, tiny animals

Animals living on land need to be able to support the weight of their own bodies. Animals living in the sea don't need to do this, as the seawater supports their weight. This means that some sea animals can grow to huge sizes, such as the blue whale, which can be up to 100 feet (30 meters) long.

Living in seawater can also mean that animals can be fragile and delicate, with no **skeleton** inside or hard shell outside. They float along, supported by the water.

DID YOU KNOW?

Fish use a side-to-side motion to swim through water. Whales, dolphins, and porpoises use an up-and-down motion. This is because they have **evolved**, over millions of years, from being mammals that lived on land. These ancient mammals used their limbs in an up-and-down motion.

This comb jellyfish has very thin body parts, which you can see right through.

Deep-sea life

It is totally dark in the deep sea. There are no plants growing here for animals to eat, so animals living here are **carnivores**, which eat other animals, and **scavengers**, which eat dead things. Some deep-sea animals can produce light, using chemicals in their bodies. This is called bioluminescence. They use this light to attract mates for breeding, and also to attract prey.

Anglerfish live in the deep sea. Part of their spine has adapted to form a long pole, which it dangles in front of its mouth. This attracts prey, which is caught and held fast by the backward-pointing teeth.

Living around the coast

There is a huge area of coastline around the world, where the sea covers the land for part of the day. The rest of the day the land is uncovered. This is called the **intertidal zone**.

Seaweeds and animals living in the intertidal zone need special adaptations to cope with these changing conditions. When the tide is in, they need to cope with the pounding of waves and the movement of water. When the tide is out, they need to cope with evaporation, and with the sun's heat.

Some seaweeds, such as some red seaweeds, have feathery leaves to cope with the movement of water. Brown seaweed leaves, such as those of wracks and kelps, are leathery, which stops them from drying out in the sun.

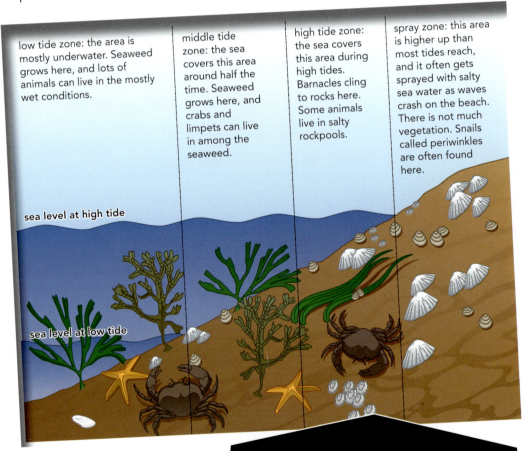

low tide zone: the area is mostly underwater. Seaweed grows here, and lots of animals can live in the mostly wet conditions.

middle tide zone: the sea covers this area around half the time. Seaweed grows here, and crabs and limpets can live in among the seaweed.

high tide zone: the sea covers this area during high tides. Barnacles cling to rocks here. Some animals live in salty rockpools.

spray zone: this area is higher up than most tides reach, and it often gets sprayed with salty sea water as waves crash on the beach. There is not much vegetation. Snails called periwinkles are often found here.

sea level at high tide

sea level at low tide

Plants and animals at the sea-end of intertidal zones are the least well adapted to living out of seawater. Those at the land-end are the most well adapted.

Intertidal animals

Animals such as crabs and sea snails hide under thick mats of seaweed at low tide. Limpets and barnacles stick to rocks, and only feed and breed in the short time they are covered by the sea.

On muddy beaches animals such as razor clams and lugworms burrow down into the mud. When the tide is high, they stick tubes called **siphons** into the water to catch food.

Eureka moment!

Scientists believe they can use some shellfish to check levels of pollution in the sea. In 2004, they discovered that growth rings on the shells of cockles and mussels can trap pollution in them. They hope to use this information to see how pollution levels in the sea change over time.

Mussels such as these shown here are found most frequently in the low and middle intertidal zones.

What Are Predator and Prey Adaptations?

Predators are animals that hunt other animals, then eat them. The animals they hunt are called prey. Predators have adaptations to help them catch their prey. Prey animals have adaptations to avoid being caught!

Safety in numbers

Grasslands are huge grassy plains, where lots of grazing animals live. There is often very little cover where they can hide from predators. Some animals, such as wildebeest, live together in huge groups. This gives them some protection from predators. When they are under attack, they scatter and run off in different directions. This confuses their attackers.

WHAT'S NEXT?

Barn owls hunt at night, using their excellent sense of hearing to listen for tiny animals like voles. Their wings make almost no noise, so the owls can silently swoop down on their prey. Engineers are now looking at the design of their wings, to develop aircraft wings that let air pass over them more smoothly.

Some predators, like these African wild dogs, also live in groups. They work together in a hunt to surround and catch their prey.

Adapted to hunt

Predators usually have very good **senses**, especially eyesight, hearing, and smell. Some are very fast and strong. Many have sharp claws, teeth, or beaks to catch, kill, and eat their prey.

Some animals **ambush** their prey. They lie in wait, often camouflaged, until their prey is close to them. Then they pounce swiftly to catch their prey. Some animals, such as snakes and spiders, use **venom** to kill prey. Others use traps, and lie in wait for their prey to get caught.

Many types of spiders weave webs to catch and trap their prey.

Evading capture

Prey animals have several clever ways of avoiding being caught by predators. Many of them use camouflage to blend into the background. Some use speed and **stamina** to simply outrun their predators.

Some animals that can't run or fly away use chemicals against their predators. Many caterpillars taste unpleasant, so birds learn not to eat them. Some animals do more than taste bad—they are poisonous. Some, like the poison-arrow frog, are very brightly colored. This is a way of advertising their poison, so animals don't even try to eat them.

Some lizards shed their tails if they are attacked. The tail carries on wriggling for a while, distracting the predator while the lizard escapes. The lizard then grows a new tail.

When leafy sea dragons swim among seaweed, their amazing camouflage makes them very difficult for predators to spot.

Super senses

Many prey animals need to look and listen out for predators all the time. They have eyes on the sides of their heads, so they can see what is around them as well as in front. They have large ears that can turn toward sounds. Some, such as meerkats, live in large groups. They can take turns watching out for predators, and can warn the others if one is near.

Eureka moment!

In the nineteenth century, a scientist named H. W. Bates discovered that some animals pretend to be poisonous, for example by having bright colors. In fact they are not poisonous, but predators leave them alone!

The peacock butterfly flashes open its wings if a predator gets near. The large spots look like the eyes of a larger animal. The predator is startled, and this gives the butterfly time to fly away.

Try This!

Many prey animals need to use camouflage to hide from their predators. Try this experiment in a group to see how well color camouflage works.

Prediction

Green-colored toothpicks hidden in a yard will be more difficult to find than red, yellow, and blue toothpicks.

What you need

- wooden toothpicks
- green, yellow, red, and blue paint
- pens or dye
- pencil and paper

What you do

1 Color 20 toothpicks, 5 in each color: green, yellow, red, and blue.

2 One of your group needs to go in the yard. They must place the toothpicks in and around any green plants, scattering them throughout an area no larger than 16 feet by 16 feet (5 meters by 5 meters).

3 Now the rest of your group needs to find as many toothpicks as possible! They should have a time limit for their search. Perhaps start with a one-minute search, and add another minute or two if they are struggling to find any toothpicks.

4 Once the time limit is up, gather all the toothpicks that the group has found. Sort them into colored piles—green, red, yellow, and blue.

5 Count the number of toothpicks in each pile. What do you notice about the number of green toothpicks compared to the other colors?

Conclusion
The group found fewer green toothpicks because they were better camouflaged against the green plants.

How Do Living Things Cope with Extreme Environments?

Some places on Earth have very extreme conditions, and it is difficult for almost all living things to exist there. For example, some lakes have very high levels of minerals in them, making them very salty.

Mono Lake in California is almost three times as salty as the sea. A plant called pickleweed lives above the shoreline. It removes salt from the water it takes in, and stores the salt in special places in its **cells**. It can then use the water, with the salt removed.

WHAT'S NEXT?

Water bears are tiny bugs. In very dry conditions, they have adapted to drying out completely. They can exist in this death-like state for years, until the environment gets wet again. They can even survive in space! Scientists want to study them to discover how they could protect other living things from extreme environments.

Surviving habitat destruction

Sometimes habitats can be completely destroyed, for example after a volcanic eruption, forest fire, or landslide. The land left behind is often bare, and new plants and animals can start to move in. Plants whose seeds are adapted to being blown by the wind are often the first to grow in bare soil. Plants adapted to growing on bare rocks are the first to grow in areas where there is no soil.

The first plants to grow in an area change the habitat by breaking down the rock and rotting. This means other plants can start to grow there.

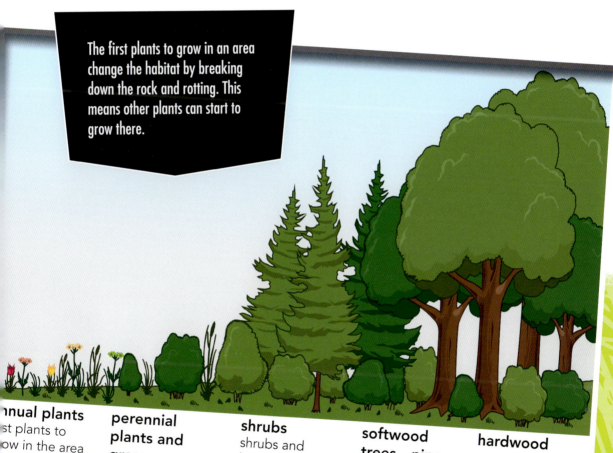

annual plants
first plants to grow in the area help to break up the rock

perennial plants and grasses
longer-living plants and grasses can grow after the first plants have changed the habitat a bit

shrubs
shrubs and bushes take a bit longer to grow, but they begin to shade out the smaller plants

softwood trees—pines
fast-growing trees like pines grow among the shrubs

hardwood trees
slow-growing trees eventually shade out other trees and some of the smaller plants

Living in urban areas

Humans manage to live in almost every habitat on Earth. We have done this by using technological adaptations to help us survive. For example, we use clothes and heating for warmth, tools and chemicals for producing food, buildings for shelter, and engines for travel. We even manage to live in space, using life-support systems in a completely hostile environment.

We have changed large areas of Earth by living there. However, many plants and animals have adapted to living in **urban** environments. Often we think of these plants and animals as pests, and try to control their numbers.

Lots of household waste ends up in large garbage dumps. Seagulls flock to these dumps, where they feed on scraps of food.

Urban animals

Rats are very well adapted to living around humans. They eat almost anything that we leave lying around. Spiders, cockroaches, and flies like living in houses. Flies and cockroaches eat our food, and spiders eat flies and cockroaches.

Pigeons and seagulls live in towns and cities, eating scraps of food from trash cans and the ground. Foxes, badgers, raccoons, and skunks also like to eat our waste food. In some areas, bears wander into towns, causing a problem for the people living there.

DID YOU KNOW?

The number of honeybees around the world is falling. However, flowers in urban areas are attracting honeybees into towns and cities. More and more people in urban areas are now keeping beehives and making honey.

Raccoons are clever enough to open and tip over many trash cans in towns and cities.

Adapting and Surviving

Across Earth, there are hundreds of thousands of different plants and animals, all adapted to surviving in different environments. They have all changed over time, as their habitats have changed. Plants and animals that were living on Earth millions of years ago are no longer found on Earth, as conditions have changed and living things have adapted.

Losing habitats

As humans use more and more of Earth's **resources** and land, habitats are being destroyed and lost. This means that we are losing many types of plants and animals forever. They simply can't adapt quickly enough to survive in the new environments.

Huge amounts of rain forest trees are being cut down and used as wood. Rain forest plants and animals can't adapt quickly enough to this massive change, and many are becoming extinct.

upsetting the balance

Plants and animals in a habitat exist together. When we start to lose one type of plant or animal, it can have a big effect on another. For example, pandas mostly eat bamboo. If bamboo died out, pandas would either have to adapt to eating something else, or die. We should try to save as many different plants and animals as we can, to keep Earth's amazing diversity.

Eureka moment!

In 1992 researchers discovered a new antelope-like animal called a saola in Vietnam. It is related to cattle, but looks like an antelope. It was the first large mammal to be discovered in over 50 years. It is extremely secretive and rare, and researchers still have much to learn about its behavior. Vietnamese conservation groups are trying hard to protect saola from dying out.

The Queen of the Andes is a plant that blooms and makes seeds only once in the 80 to 100 years that it lives. This means that the plant is very slow to adapt to changing conditions. It is now listed as endangered.

Glossary

adapt change to suit surroundings

ambush to make a surprise attack from a hidden place

amphibian small animal that spends part of its life cycle in water and part of its life cycle on land

biome large area of the earth, characterized by a similar climate and conditions

camouflage way of hiding by blending into the surroundings

carnivore animal that eats only meat

cell tiny part of human or plant life

climate usual weather conditions in a place

diverse varied

evaporate to turn from liquid into gas

evergreen type of tree or plant that does not lose its leaves in the winter

evolve to develop

foothills lower hills near the base of a mountain or mountains

gills organs for breathing used by fish and other animals that live in water

global warming general increase in the world's temperatures, which many scientists believe is caused by human pollution

habitat place where an animal lives

holdfast root-like plant structure by which some seaweeds attach themselves to rocks

intertidal zone area of a shore between the high-tide and low-tide marks

mammal warm-blooded animal with fur or hair and a skeleton inside its body. Female mammals produce milk to feed their babies. Humans are mammals.

migrate to move to another region, usually in search of food or warmer weather

mineral substance that we get from food. Some are important for keeping us healthy.

natural selection process by which those animals that are best suited to their environment survive and reproduce, while others gradually die off

oxygen gas in the air, needed by most living things for survival

predator animal that hunts other animals for food

prey animal that is hunted by another

resource source of help or information

scavenger animal that finds and eats dead animals or rotting plants

senses ways in which we understand our surroundings. The five senses are sight, hearing, smell, taste, and touch.

siphon tube or pipe used to suck liquid

skeleton framework of bones inside an animal's body

stamina strength to keep up an activity over a long period

stem main part of a plant that grows up from the ground and supports leaves, flowers, fruit, or branches

summit peak or top of a mountain

urban to do with towns and cities

venom poison

Find Out More

Books

Biskup, Agniesezka. *A Journey into Adaptation with Max Axiom, Super Scientist*. Mankato, Minn.: Capstone, 2007.

Spilsbury, Richard. *Adaptation and Survival*. New York: Rosen, 2010.

Walker, Denise. *Adaptation and Survival*. New York: M. Evans and Company, 2010.

Web sites

http://education.nationalgeographic.com/education/encyclopedia/adaptation/?ar_a=1

This National Geographic site has information about animal and plant adaptations based on their environment. You can also see pictures of specific species and learn how they've uniquely adapted to their circumstances.

www.bbc.co.uk/bitesize/ks2/science/living_things/plant_animal_habitats/read/1/

On this BBC educational site you can read about habitats and adaptations, play a plant and animal habitats game, and do a quiz to test yourself!

www.coolantarctica.com/Antarctica%20fact%20file/wildlife/antarctic_animal_adaptations.htm

On this web site you can find out about lots of adaptations that help animals living in the Antarctic.

http://teacher.scholastic.com/dirtrep/animal/invest.htm

If you would like to do some investigations about what adaptations animals in your local area have, you can use the sheets here to record your findings. There is also some information about various animals and their adaptations.

Places to visit

There are many great science museums around the United States—maybe there's one near you! The Museum of Life and Science in Durham, North Carolina, is a good example. It has more than 75 animal species and includes a butterfly house and insectarium. You can learn about how plants and animals have changed over time, and separate the predators from the prey!

Go for a walk in your local nature park! Spend time looking closely at all the different plants you can see. Sit quietly and see how many animals you spot. Notice how different plants and animals are adapted to this habitat.

Organizations to contact

Friends of the Earth
This organization campaigns for solutions to environmental problems. They want to protect Earth, for people and wildlife to live better together.

World Wildlife Fund (WWF)
This is an organization set up in 1961. It aims to protect the diversity of plants and animals around the world. They campaign for less pollution and better use of resources, and other ways of reducing the human impact on Earth.

Zoological Association of America (ZAA)
The ZAA promotes the conservation of animals and the proper care, safety, and quality of conditions for animals in captive environments, such as zoos.

Further research

There is a lot more information about adaptation you could find out about. What interests you most about adaptation? Do you want to discover how plants and animals have adapted over time? Or do you want to find out about some clever adaptations that plants and animals have?

Index